WORLD DANCE SERIES
MEXICAN FOLK DANCES
WITH CD ACCOMPANIMENT, EASY TO FOLLOW DANCE GRAPHICS, ORFF & PERCUSSION ARRANGEMENTS

CONTENTS

Art: Odalis Soto
Editor: Debbie Cavalier
Production Coordinator: Diane Laucirica

Instrumental Arrangements by
EDWARD B. JUREY, Music Consultant, Los Angeles City Schools.
MARIA ARIAS CRUZ, Leader of Maria Cruz Orchestra

ISBN 0-89898-947-7

9 780898 989472

1. La Raspa

FORMATION: Partners facing, hands joined, arms outstretched, in a double circle, men's backs to the center.

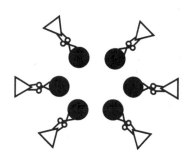

INTRODUCTION - Three Beats

DANCE DIRECTIONS:

RASPA STEP (Theme A in the music)

Count 1 — Jump in place to "stride" position, right foot forward, toes up

Count 2 — Again jump in place, this time placing left foot forward, toes up.

Count 3 — Again jump in place, right foot forward.

Count 4 — Hold position — don't move!

   (Repeat these steps but begin the LEFT FOOT FORWARD this time)

   (Repeat again beginning with the left foot)

   (Repeat)

Cue Step:	count 1	ct 2	ct 3	ct 4
	Jump right,	left,	right,	hold
	Jump left,	right,	left,	hold
	Jump right,	left,	right,	hold
	Jump left,	right,	left,	hold.

CHORUS: (THEME B)

Partners LINK RIGHT ELBOWS and do 8 SKIP STEPS around each other.

Then reverse direction, LINKING LEFT ELBOWS, and do 8 SKIP STEPS around each other.

(Repeat the above, linking right then left elbows).

THE MUSIC REPEATS THREE MORE TIMES AND YOU MAY SIMPLY USE THE SAME TWO STEPS FOR THE REMAINDER OF THE RECORDING.

HERE ARE SOME VARIATIONS YOU MAY WISH TO TRY.

VARIATIONS FOR THE RASPA STEP:

1. On the jump, place the feet sideward instead of forward.

2. Or cross one foot in front of the other on the jump.

3. Partners drop hands, and when doing the jumps, turn the body so that first the left shoulders are toward each other then right, then left.

VARIATIONS FOR THE CHORUS:

Do the right, left, right, left elbow swings as before, but on each change of elbow and direction the boy takes a new partner (moving counterclockwise around the circle to take the new partner), and on each group of 8 skips the partners make one complete circle around each other. The boy thus swings his partner and then three more girls in succession, taking the last girl as his new partner for the RASPA STEP that follows.

2. La Bamba

FORMATION: LA BAMBA is performed in lines, boys in one line, girls in another, facing each other about 10 feet apart. The foot sounds are an important part of the dance, so there is as little motion as possible in the upper part of the body. Hands hang at the sides and the shoulders are straight.

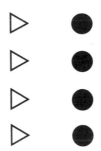

LA BAMBA STEP

Count 1 — Slide right foot forward (small steps always, keeping feet on floor).

Count 2 — Slide left foot forward.

Count 3 — Slide right foot forward.

Count 4 — Keeping weight on right foot, hop on that foot at the same time dragging it back (a chug step). In the next measure start with the left foot, and so on, alternating throughout the dance.

SIMPLIFIED BAMBA STEP: Same as above, but on the count of 4, PAUSE (do not do the chug step).

Cue Step: Right, Left, Right, Hold
            Left, Right, Left, Hold, etc.

COUNT I   **COUNT 2**

COUNT 3   **COUNT 4**

DANCE DIRECTIONS

Introduction — Stand motionless

FIGURE I

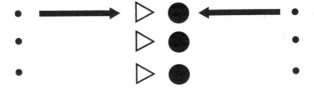

Both lines advance toward center.

2 bamba steps (Starting R, then L, then R, then L)

Both lines move backward to place,

2 bamba steps (Starting R, then L, then R, then L)

FIGURE II

Girls' line advances to boys' line.

8 bamba steps.

Girls' line backward to place.

8 bamba steps

FIGURE III

Boys' line advance to girls' line.
   8 bamba steps
Boys' line, backward to place.
   8 bamba steps
(When the boys' or girls' line is not moving, the bamba step is done in place, continuously.)

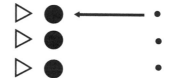

FIGURE IV

Both lines advance to center and pass through, 8 bamba
   steps to opposite side, and turn to face center.
   (Right shoulder to right shoulder with partner.)
Repeat Figure IV — returning to original place,
   8 bamba steps.

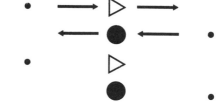

FIGURE V

Both lines advance to center with 4 steps. Partners circle
   each other (to r. shoulder) — with 4 steps.
Continue to opposite lines in 4 steps.
Repeat Figure V — returning to original place.
   (12 steps)

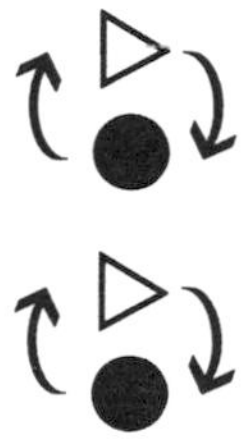

FIGURE VI

Both lines advance to center in 2 steps, then facing
   front in one long line, girl in front of partner.
Single line moves forward.
As dancers reach front of line, girls circle wide to their
   right, and boys circle wide to their left.
                              16 bamba steps

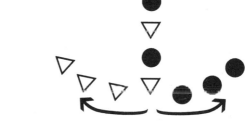

FIGURE VII

Partners meet, where back end of line was, and proceed
   forward side by side, girl on right side of boy.
                              18 bamba steps

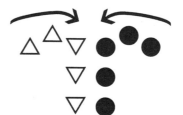

FIGURE VIII

Couples form a long single line, facing front, spread out
   side by side.

Method:
   Couple 1 stops in the middle,
   Couple 2 moves to place at R,
   Couple 3 moves to place at L,
   Couple 4 moves to place at R,
   Couple 5 moves to place at L,
   Etc. . . . (see diagram)

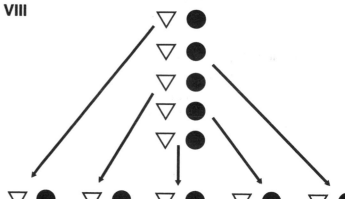

FIGURE IX

All face left and follow the leader in a serpentine column to the end of the recording.

6

3. La Cucaracha

FORMATION: Form 2 lines, boys on one side, girls on the other, partners facing, 4 or 5 feet apart. Boys clasp hands behind, the girl holds skirt out in front.

As in LA RASPA there are two distinct musical themes, which we will call A and B.

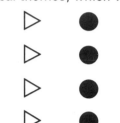

CUCARACHA STEP

Authentic:

First Measure

Count 1 — Starting with the right foot, step across in front of the left foot, turning the whole body to the left.

Count 2 — Step back on the left foot.

Count 3 — Close the right foot to the left foot

Second Measure

Count 1 — With left foot step across and in front of right foot, turning whole body to the right.

Count 2 — Step back on the right foot.

Count 3 — Close left foot to right foot.

Simplified

First Measure (3 counts) — simply step off with right foot in front of left, turning to the left (as above.)

Second Measure (3 counts) — pivot on right foot, and place left foot in front of right foot, turning whole body half way around.
(continue swinging the body once each measure as you step left then right, etc.)

Starting Position   **COUNT1**

COUNT2   **COUNT3**

DANCE DIRECTIONS
Introduction — One measure

THEME A — Do 8 Cucaracha steps in place.

THEME A — Do 8 Cucaracha steps toward your partner and circling the partner clockwise, returning to original position facing partner.

THEME B — Jump to the right with the right foot (turning in direction at the same time) and do 3 little running steps, then stamp twice with left foot. Then turn in place in 3 counts half-way around to the right with a RIGHT, LEFT, RIGHT, STAMP, STAMP (stamping with the left foot again.) Repeat this pattern and step but this time to the left, starting with the left foot.

REPEAT THIS PATTERN FOR THEME B 3 more times to complete the music for THEME B.

THEME A — Cucaracha steps in place.

THEME B — Do the same "run, run, run, stamp, stamp" pattern as in Theme B above, but do so straight ahead, lines crossing, partners crossing right shoulders and taking each other's place. Then turning in place with a RIGHT, LEFT, RIGHT (turning), STAMP, STAMP.

Repeat, this time starting with left foot, lines crossing again and returning to original positions.

REPEAT ALL OF THE ABOVE UNTIL THE MUSIC ENDS.

4. Chiapanecas
(Clap Hands Dance)

FORMATION: Couples in large double circle facing counter-clockwise, inside hands joined, girls on outside holding skirts wide with outside hand.

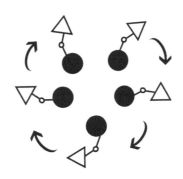

DANCE DIRECTIONS:

Introduction — Sway in place. — Four measures

Step 1.   Balance forward onto outside foot;
Balance back onto inside foot;
Balance forward onto outside foot;
Clap! Clap! and turn to face opposite direction
(Clockwise)

Repeat above step, end by turning to face partner and joining hands.

Step 2.   Balance away from partner;
Balance toward partner;
Balance away from partner;
Clap! Clap! (own hands)

Step 3.   Moving sideward CCW*, step, close; step, close;
pause; tap, tap (trailing foot).
Reverse direction, still facing partner, moving CW.**
Step, close; step, close pause; tap, tap (trailing foot).

Step 4.   With slow, sauntering walking steps, pass partner right shoulder to right shoulder, then back to back, then diagonally backward toward right, to face new partner. (This is a do-sa-do).

Repeat all, with a new partner each time.

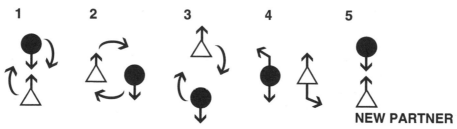

*CCW - counter clockwise **CW- clockwise

5. Chihuahua

FORMATION: Four lines of dancers, the outside columns composed of boys; the inside columns, girls 6 to 8 in each line, and dancers several feet apart in all directions. Partners are facing at the beginning; girls' hands are handling their full skirts, boys' hands are clasped behind their backs.

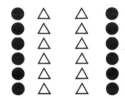

DANCE DIRECTIONS:
Introduction — Four measures

FIGURE I
(Plucked violin solo)
Girl, Then Boy Skip
Girls only dance; boys kneel on L knee, hands on hips, facing partner.
8 skips in place, facing partner
8 skips in place facing back of room
8 skips in place, facing away from partner
8 skips in place, facing front of room
REPEAT above, this time boys skipping, girls kneeling.

FIGURE II
(Bowed violin solo)
Slide Across Step
All stand and face front.
With 4 step-steps (side, close; side, close; side, close)
 partners change places, girls passing in front of
 boys and turning head to look at partners
With 4 side-steps, return to place in same manner,
 moving in opposite direction.
Repeat Figure II

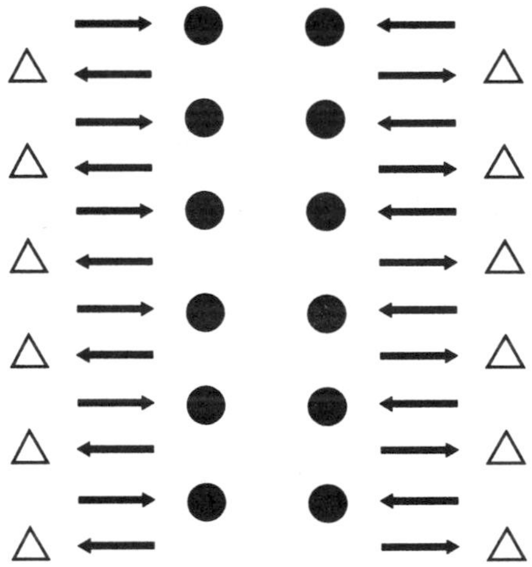

FIGURE III
(Plucked violin solo)
Chorus Skip
All skip in place, facing partner
All skip in place, facing back
All skip in place, facing away from partner
All skip in place, facing front

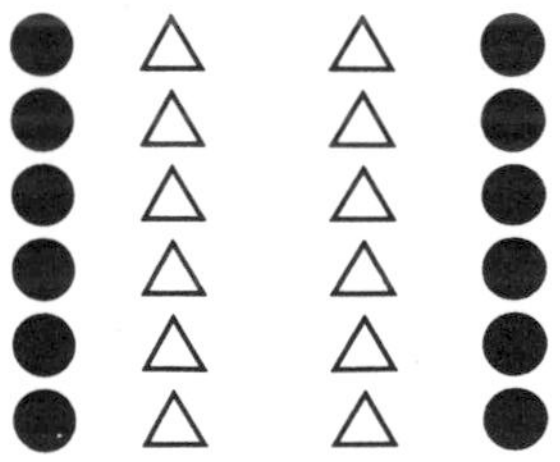

FIGURE IV
(Trumpet solo)
Follow the Leader
With 16 marching steps, starting R foot, each line follows front
 leader counter - clockwise, back along the column to the back;
 then turns and follows leader forward to starting position.
 (Each column does this independently of the others.)
Repeat Figure IV

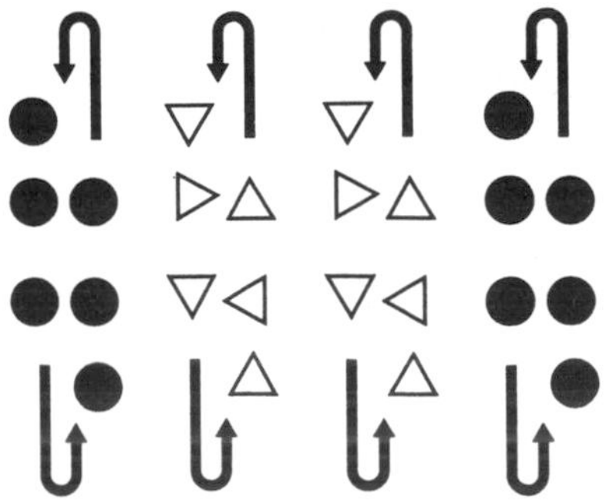

FIGURE V
(Piccolo solo)
Elbow Skip

Partners link R elbows, holding L hands high, and
skip around each other.
Reverse, linking L elbows, holding R hands high,
skipping around partner.

FIGURE VI
(Trumpet solo)
Arches

All couples form arches by joining hands. With 16 marching
steps, the head couple leads other couples back through
the arches. As each couple reaches the front they drop
hands, turn around, join hands (Boys' L. with Girls' R.),
and march back through the arches to original positions.
Drop hands and separate to be in position as at start of dance,
swaying in place.

FIGURE VII
(Plucked violin solo)
Chorus Skip

Repeat Figure III. Chorus skip:
Facing partner
Facing back
Facing away from partner
Facing front

FIGURE VIII
(Bowed violin solo)
Slide Across Step

Repeat Figure II. Change places with partner and return.
4 slide steps on way, 4 back.

FIGURE IX
(Bowed violin solo)
Chorus Skip
(faster tempo)

Repeat Figure III. Chorus skip:
Facing partner
Facing back
Facing away from partner
Facing front

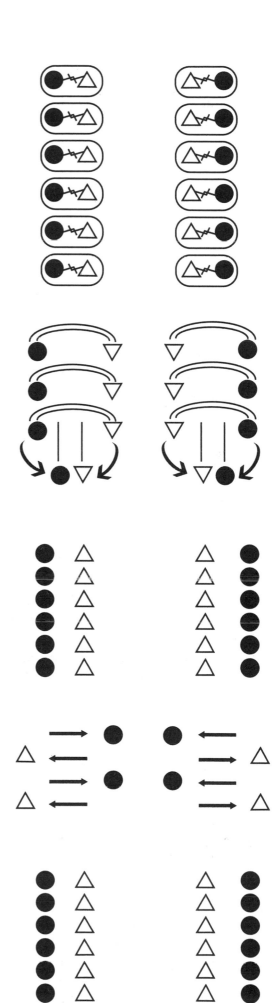

6. La Jesusita

FORMATION: Single circle. Boys clasp hands behind backs, girls hold skirts in front.

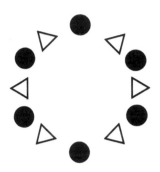

DANCE DIRECTIONS:
Introduction — Two measures

Section A — Step to the right with the right foot; step, close, step, close, step, close, step, and swing left foot over the right while hopping on right (a schottische step). Turn and repeat in opposite direction back to back.

Section B — Partners now face each other, boys on inside of circle. Starting with the right foot, skip backwards three skips and tap twice with the left toe. Then skip three steps forward and tap twice with the right toe.

REPEAT ALL OF THE ABOVE UNTIL THE MUSIC ENDS.

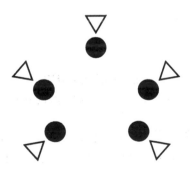

VARIATIONS FOR THEME A:
   Crossover Step — partners circle clockwise, touching right then left elbows, etc.; step with right foot in front of left turning so that partners right elbows touch; step on left foot; step on right foot, turning to right so that partners left elbows touch; step on left foot.

7. La Burrita
(The Little Donkey)

FORMATION: Partners facing same direction in a circle. Partner in back puts hands on waist of partner ahead.

Lyrics:

1. Arre, arre, arre, mi burrita, Aqui me chu, Aqui me chu.
2. Arre, arre, arre, mi burrita, Aqui me chu, Aqui me chu.
3. Now I get on my little donkey even though she is forlorn,
4. Because I did not give her alfalfa, I did not give her corn.
5. Pobrecita, mi burrita! She will show me she can balk,
6. One step forward she will take and one step backward she will walk.
7. Pobrecita, mi burrita! Don't be cross or be forlorn,
8. We will get there very soon and I am going to give you corn.

DANCE DIRECTIONS:
Introduction — Six measures

Lines 1 & 2: Three steps and a hop (8 times).
Lines 3 & 4: Partners cross hands, skip in a small circle.
Lines 5 & 6: Reverse direction, continue to skip.
Lines 7 & 8: Same as 1 & 2.

Orff and Percussion Arrangements
by Debbie Cavalier and Sandy Feldstein

ABOUT THE INSTRUMENT PARTS

Throughout the following Orff/Percussion arrangements, the indicated
instruments have characteristic sounds. Other instruments within the same
basic sound families may be added or substituted.

For example:

Maracas - Cabasa - Chocallo - other shakers
Tambourine - Hand Drum - Jingle Sticks, shaker family instruments
Claves - Wood Block - Tone Block - Rhythm Sticks
Drums (high, low) - Bongos - Hand Drum & Conga Drum - 2 Pitched Conga Drums - Thumb Piano

MEXICAN FOLK DANCES
1. LA RASPA*

*Play through three times in G, transpose up to C one time then down to F one time.

2. LA BAMBA

3. LA CUCARACHA*

*Play 2 times and transpose to C then G then C again.

BMR05117

4. LA CHIAPANECAS*

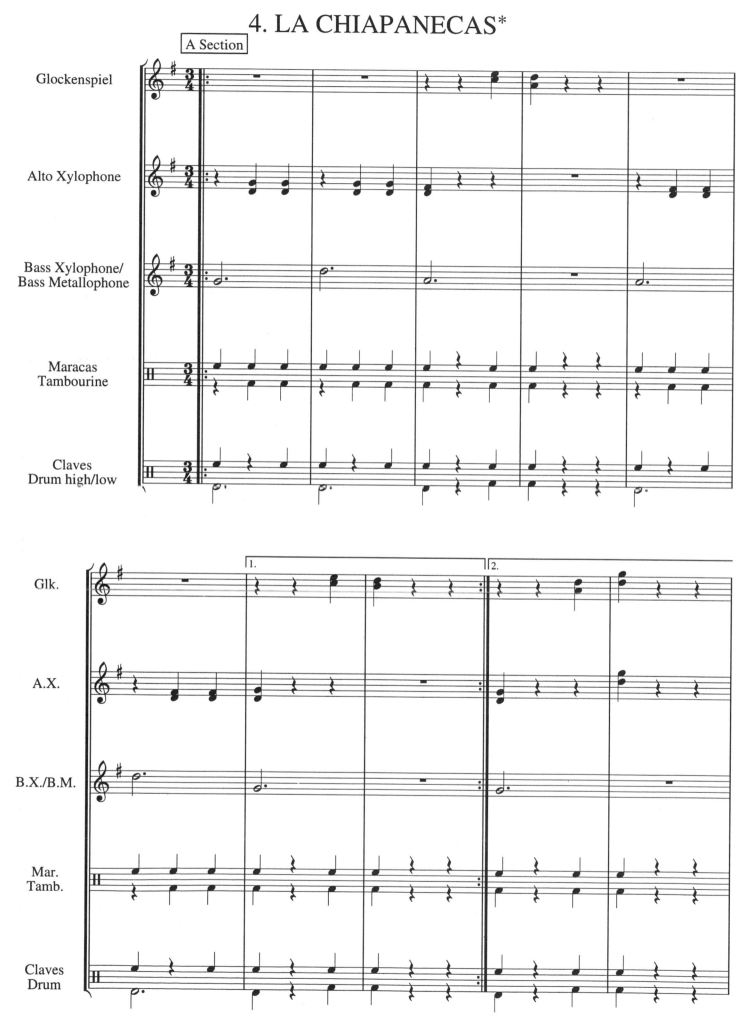

*Repeat song, then transpose to F, then to C, then back to F. The tempo increases with each repeat.

BMR05117

5. CHIHUAHUA

6. LA JESUSITA*

7. LA BURRITA

MULTICULTURAL: WORLD DANCE SERIES

The WORLD DANCE SERIES is excellent for classrooms, music programs, physical education classes, day care centers and home use. Building upon the respected Bowmar albums of folk dances, this celebration of dances around the world is being updated in graphics, sound and usability. The new editions are remastered on an accompaniment CD to upgrade sound and to provide ease of track location. The edition includes not only text but easy-to-follow dance graphics. Each package includes:

- a booklet of easy-to-follow text and dance graphics for instructional assistance
- accompaniment tracks on CD for ease of track location and clarity of sound
- cultural background and information.

Folk Dances from Around the World
__ (BMR 00114) Record $12.50*
__ (BMR 05114) Book and CD $19.95
Dance direction by Fredericka Moore. Edited by Bryce Bowmar. Eight traditional folk dances including the Sicilian Circle, Military Schottische and the Virginia Reel. Grades 2-6

Folk Dances of Hawaii
__ (BMR 00116) Record $12.50*
__ (BMR 05116) Book and CD $19.95
Ethnic Hawaiian dance patterns by Sylvia Marks and Valerie Sill. Authentic and beautiful music performed by South Sea Islanders. Grades 4-7

Folk Dances of Latin America
__ (BMR 00115) Record $12.50*
__ (BMR 05115) Book and CD $19.95
Dance direction by Fredericka Moore. Edited by Bryce Bowmar. Includes folk dances from Argentina, Venezuela, Panama and Brazil. Grades 5-8

Mexican Folk Dances
__ (BMR 05117) Book and CD $19.95
Traditional Mexican favorites including La Bamba, La Cucaracha and many more. Grades 2-6

*A limited number of original LP editions are available.

bowmar